Secretary of the Invisible Thing

Lance Larsen

Rattle | Studio City, California | 2026

Secretary of the Invisible Thing

Layout and design by Timothy Green

Cover art by Lance Larsen
"Vigil," 2026 (Photo by Jacqui Larsen)

ISBN: 978-1-931307-66-6

First edition

Rattle Foundation
12411 Ventura Blvd
Studio City, CA 91604
www.rattle.com

Contents

Secretary *of the* Invisible Thing

The world is the closed door. It is a barrier.
And at the same time it is the way through.

—*Simone Weil*

One's ignorance is one's chief asset.

—*Wallace Stevens*

Here's a truck stop instead of St. Peter's.

—*R.E.M.*

Sitting on a Bench, I Doze Off Piecing Together the Day

Let's see, just after lunch I turned a blind corner
and lucked into a Banksy. "Hammer Boy,"
it's called, a shadow of a tike taking a sledge
to an actual hydrant. It's on West 79th behind
plexiglass. I felt instantly famous among bricks
and pulsing sky. Before that, a street bagel.
Before that, I passed a woman, on the sidewalk,
reading braille, fingers fluttering in another
world. I felt bad twice. First for having so much
change, second for dropping too much in her
coffee can. Her yellow lab was breathtaking,
teeth like a prayer, spiky collar like many
answers. Before that, I crossed Brooklyn Bridge
and learned it takes workers twelve years
to paint it, which kicked me, who knows why,
into high gear. Before that I woke in a sublet
I was renting from someone's cousin and ate
cold Kung Pao to keep breakfast quiet.
Before that, it was the night before and I
was walking 5th Avenue, thinking, not only
am I an orphan at home but here on vacation.
How, how can I send a selfie to my dead?
Before that, a gang of fireflies in Central
Park blinking on and off: look at them, how
accidentally beautiful, on and off, like
Thelonious Monk, in clubs dotting Harlem,
plunking out God with all those wrong notes.

Interior Weather

I prefer to sip but like keeping company with those who chug.
I prefer help blowing out candles.
I prefer the day before Christmas, the day after Halloween.
I prefer the angel with a badly chipped wing.
I prefer a clear exit strategy.
I prefer hearing a barn owl to seeing a barn owl.
I prefer Chagall's floating peasants, who seem to rise on fugitive kisses.
I prefer dashes and stars in the margin, maybe hints of a grocery list.
I prefer grottos licked by light.
I prefer toy guns, the kind that shoot water or light cigars,
    especially on balconies perfumed by the sea.
I prefer *discombobulated* and *skittywampus*. Also *Oy!*
I prefer rope swings on stage and water dripping.
I prefer taking the mulligan, whether I need it or not.
I prefer shopkeepers who ignore me.
I prefer decorating trees with mantises and small skulls.
I prefer hopping around in collections, cricket style, so I never
    know what I've come to the end of.
I prefer passwords with a dead pet buried in the middle.
I prefer shaggy run-ons and chancy, giddyap, skips of syntax.
I prefer freshly squeezed lime.
I prefer *Rats live on no evil star* over *Able was I ere I saw Elba.*
I prefer hangdog, backsliding prophets like Jonah.
I prefer irony, except when holy-cow earnestness saves the day.
I prefer psalms sung by insects, their dusky improvisations.
I prefer to spring forward rather than fall back.
I prefer to float.
I prefer not knowing the *when* or the *where.*
I prefer turning each delicate 8 on its side and calling it infinity.

after "Possibilities" by Wisława Szymborska

Lives of the Animals

Remember how frogs wise as Aquinas spawned
in musky ponds, and you licked
butterfly dust off your fingers for luck?
Remember hopping rabbits, each one
a manifesto in white, how when you napped,
they opened their pink eyes inside you?
Remember that invisible kingdom
assembling behind your solar plexus,
leaf by feather by haunting ghost,
like a nest, and this is where your soul slept?
Remember the forbidden ditch
beyond your house? After wading,
you'd peel squirming leeches from your
sister's legs, and she'd peel them from yours,
a theology of touch uniting you against
cascading dark. Remember praying
to a fox and three hours later God
would fall from the sky, splashing
everywhere, forgiving even the little things?
Remember learning the dead man's float
at the YMCA, always wondering
will there be a final test, will my held
breath float me to the other side?
Remember touching a blue-bellied lizard
and asking which shining creature
will I become in the next world?
Remember the startled magpie that flew
up and away on a winter walk, cawing,
all prodigal selves speaking your name at once?

Secretary of the Invisible Thing

This is the exact phrase Milosz uses to describe
himself and other poets, not one
who dictates but one who takes dictation,
who eavesdrops on seraphs and crooked
weather and the Zeitgeist and holds it
inside for later. If you dance with
the invisible thing, they call it the tarantella.

If you rub the bumps of the invisible thing
found on someone's head, phrenology.
Some go bowling on Taco Tuesday
to knock down invisible things everywhere,
pins glowing green like squirrels after Chernobyl.
In fifth grade I received a chain letter.
If I broke it, the invisible thing threatened

to hurt my family, especially my little sister,
but if I did as instructed, I would receive
77 postcards from Tahiti. My sister
caught the mumps, and I'm still waiting
for a flood of hula girls and exotic stamps.
Was I deceived by the invisible thing?
Maybe, but when the invisible thing gets loose,

anything can happen, maybe group meditation
in an aspen grove at Burning Man,
maybe a restraining order in a trailer park
on the edge of Fresno. I knew a busboy
who ate cold fries off a girl's plate to get close
to her spit. I knew a woman who left open
Bibles around her bed to scare off ghosts.

Both, I swear, were secretaries in training.
Once in the Rothko Chapel, I dozed
off, waking not to black panels
but the invisible thing inside me: a kaleidoscopic
pulsing that won't stop, not even when
my body stops. I'm haunted by so many
things. By wrecked cars and black holes,

by the older brother my mother miscarried,
by ragged beauty everywhere. By my daughter's
toddler, Jojo, in my kitchen sink waving
goodbye to draining bathwater, whirlpool
as elegy. But how to define the invisible
thing, a magnetic north we're hardwired
to follow? A vector, a voice without a mouth?

William Blake used to wander his garden
naked. The question isn't *Did Blake really see*
angels in his apple tree? but *Why can't we?*
My face is flushed, I'm a house on fire,
a burning no thermometer can read.
Whatever you are, whoever I'm taking
dictation from, take your time putting me out.

To My Daughter's Dead Name

Here I am sorting old documents after breakfast.
And here you are—bright as a bee sting!—
clinging to my daughter's souvenir birth certificate
three decades old. How bold you seem, Dead
Name, anchoring dates. How bold, corroborating
vitals: 21 inches, 8 pounds 3 ounces, male, etc.
How bold, floating above her tiny footprints.

Of course, I love my daughter and her new
name. But I still have a reluctant soft spot
for you, splashed with myth as you are, citizen
of the sea, the green of Wales poking through.
Now you are cipher and palimpsest, collateral
damage, slippage of signifier and signified.
Syllables we've scrubbed from our vocabulary.

To show solidarity with her, maybe I should
bury the birth certificate, along with her old
report cards, along with you, out back.
Dead Name, I swear it's nothing personal.
Dead Name, we selected you from a cast
of thousands. Dead Name, truth is I rarely think
of you till one of your accidental appearances.

Like today. Or like last fall, first day of class.
I found myself reading you, Dead Name,
from a list of hopefuls wanting to add. I paused.
Almost couldn't say you, like I was dropping
F-bombs to welcome the class. Said you
anyway. Your wild syllables waiting to home
to whoever raised their hand and said *I'm here.*

Bring Me a Horse

Instead of bending spoons with thought, we broke
popsicle sticks with our thumbs. We lacked beards,
so we slathered our faces in mayo and shaved
with butter knives. This was called tasting the world
with our skin, and this was called happiness times ten.

Someday we might need a hefty supply of poison,
so we peed in a wine bottle and added Tabasco
and dirt and dead crickets and let it cook in the sun.
We blew up anthills to prove we weren't wimps,
stuck pins in our palms to prove we weren't ghosts.

We spoke Pig Latin at lunch and tried
summoning the dead in our underground fort.
This was called speaking in tongues, and this
was called hocus-pocus for novices. Then Ty's dad died.
At the viewing, I touched his hands and thought:

he has no blood, has no blood, has no blood Possibilities" ...
And that night those of us who still had fathers
visited the river and no matter what we asked,
it grumbled the same sumpy answer: *I'm tired of spiders*
and flies, bring me a horse, a horse, a big black horse.

This was called listening to the gods,
and this was called how to keep our dads
alive and cussing. Instead, we found a rusty car
in a field and popped it out of gear and pushed
it over the bank. It splashed, then gurgled and glugged

its way to the muddy bottom. And the river
absolved us, rain kissing our heads all the way home.

Dear First Draft of This Poem

I wrote you by hand but can barely read you now.
What beautiful cross-outs you offer
the world! Is that a comma or a smeared gnat?
I wanted to stay in you forever.
Six months later, in the teeth of winter,
you seem freshly naive. Elegy and carpe diem
competing in a lovely word salad, no need

to explain what Wile E. Coyote in stanza 1
has to do with Grandpa Mac wearing nothing
but scraps of steam and floating like balsa
in stanza 3. Mark this: I felt young in you.
And deliciously irresponsible. In your margin,
a list: bread, peaches, tofu, Kalamata olives,
chips, cat food, donut holes, lemon curd ...

Was I going shopping later or imagining
Emily Dickinson hanging a left at Mount
Holyoke for a stop at Market Basket?
I have no idea. Here I go again, talking to paper.
You were greedy to include everything:
Ariadne's red thread, Sartre hiding
in his sister's closet after he won the Nobel,

a scared hamster. Let some later me
decide what stays. Until then, help me
translate a few phrases. *Kaleidoscopic arcs
of water,* were they meant to be sprinklers?
Telestial gods: sparrow hawks slicing the sky
into a playground of above and below? As for
the hamster: not mine but Nick Thomas's.

We found her after school fat with the babies
she had devoured, except for a tidy pile
of tails and feet. Is that your key trauma,
First Draft? Or me seeing my mom naked
a few lines later? I wish you'd help me
make up my mind. In you, First Draft,
I have just been born and I'll never die.

In you, everything was still possible.
In you, I tried not to care about symbols.
The sun was literally going down. Wisps
of mist, aspen leaves quavering. Magpie
doing clever magpie things on a fence.
I was almost happy. When I closed my eyes,
flecks of blue coalesced then began to rise.

AD&D

As in accidental death and dismemberment,
as in the insurance policy *The Idaho State Journal*
took out on me, their newest paperboy,
including a number I could call if I lost a limb.
Suppose a neighbor's stray arrow took
out my eye, $5,000. Suppose Old Lady
Allsop tripped while mowing and her rogue
Toro chewed off my foot, $7,500.
What a leaky, blood-filled boy I was,
a walking accident worth tens of thousands.
Haunted by mishap, I trudged, tasting gore
in every sunset, picturing compound
fractures when I crossed the screaming road.
I threw smudgy bad news six days a week,
ads heavy as Sunday, with a secret cache
of rubber bands that would last till
Armageddon. And I did my own weird
math as I walked, bartering my body
for the untouched world. With my toe,
I could buy a raging river, with my wrist
a mountain fat with elk. A rib for a waterfall,
an elbow for a lake. A crushed testicle,
wasn't that enough pain to buy Yellowstone?
What a blessed horror I was, as I zombied
along, under trees, one minute dragging
a bum leg, the next swinging an arm
I might lose by dawn. And what spying
glimpses I took in through open drapes.
A woman shaving her poodle, a man trying on
his dead wife one curly-headed wig
at a time. Ecstatic sadness in shades of blonde.

A Partial Accounting

I can name *monkshood* and *monkeyflower* and *fireweed*
but can't tell the difference between
a hurtling satellite and the entrance to heaven.
I'm jealous of smokers, who conduct
affairs of fire so close to their faces.
Robert Kennedy stumped in my hometown
three days before his assassination.
My sister got his autograph, I played ping-pong.
I've never touched an iceberg. I keep string
and string theory in the same crammed
kitchen drawer behind my eyes. I am a country
with weak borders, my quiet dead
always passing through me, advocates and avatars.
Bird song is fine, but it's bossa nova
I listen to over breakfast. What is a poem
but a lucky layover in Cleveland or Byzantium?
I prefer naps that leave sand in my hair,
or bits of dead grass. I swim but swimming
doesn't take the ache away. I still have wisdom
teeth—in a jar, which I shake like a maraca.
With an Isla del Sol shaman, I once
rowed to an energy field in Lake Titicaca.
Un punto energético, he said, *un punto sagrado.*
Then we threw yarrow and coca leaves
and prayed to dreaming gods of the dark waves.
I read tattered diaries like scripture,
the sky as an owner's manual, my bank
statement as a modern-day whodunit.
Sometimes I juggle. I hold funerals
for robins that crash into glass on my watch.
I used to carry kids on my shoulders.
Now they knock at my door and I buy their weak
lemonade and friendship bracelets. I wish
I lived on Utopia Parkway like Joseph Cornell.

Things I'm Against

Against cotton candy, against fake flowers
at graves and cars painted orange,
though I love that same shade in parrots
and tangerines. Against windmills
and microwaves, against white shoes
and season tickets to anything,
against rhubarb, against hockey,
with apologies to my new Canuck son-in-law.

Not a big fan of golf though I love the word
mulligan, oozy with second chances. I'll take
a mulligan on my last sprinkler repair,
on my write-in vote for Beyoncé,
on time-share condos. I'm pro-oxygen
and gravity and capillary action but against
the Northern Lights (they jack you up
with optimism, sure, but it never lasts).

I used to sing the sleekness of wasps
till I saw one lay a clutch of eggs inside
a living caterpillar, thus giving hatching
larvae plenty to nosh on from day one
(not on my front porch you don't!).
Against Pin-the-tail-on-the-donkey
though I loved moony, half-loony
Mrs. Luanna Lallitan, who baked money

into birthday cupcakes, devil's food
clinging to filthy dimes and nickels
and please please please let my secret
coin be a quarter. I'm usually against
Shelley, sometimes Wordsworth,
never against Keats (unless you count
Endymion), and happy beyond measure
for the spiky-haired goth girl in Rome

who selected a pea-sized pebble
from Keats' grave, rinsed it in iced tea,
then popped it into her mouth
like ecstasy. I'm against armed robbery,
even petty theft (who isn't?) but love
the story of the phantom crew
two towns away who stole over 40,000
apples from an orchard in one night.

Think of it: a dozen pickers, a giant truck
or two, banks of lights, maybe a generator.
That's a lot of chutzpah and organization
and Cosmic Crisps to cram in your
pockets. Of course, I'm against cancer,
especially brain cancer, which did
a number on Skye, age three, next door.
Her six-year-old sister said, *Why in a grave?*

Can't we just keep her in the corner
in the playroom and change her hat
each morning? Against seances too,
all those fake ghost voices, but all-in
on impromptu chats with the dead,
especially my dad. Why didn't you make me
go fishing with you? I would have picked
it up. Teach me to tie a sheepshank.

How should I read this hatch? I know
you're listening. Why won't you interfere
in my life? Tell me again how it felt
to pass through the Panama locks
on a destroyer on Christmas Eve?
When will you pass through me?
Bring your whetstone, show me how to spit
on knives and bring an edge to every rusty blade.

Custodian of Scat

I've freed a baby quail that fell into a window well,
saved a garter snake from a prowling stray.

And just now, quite by accident, I lent my elbow
to a spider building a flimsy condo out of silk and air.

All this in a single week. What's next—re-hang
these fallen leaves? Erase trails of drunken snails?

With a stingy kiss, pollinate a rose? I'm tired, Lord.
For decades now I've dragged this drippy hose

to thirsty plants. How long must I remain dean
of root and spore, custodian of scat, before you take

me home? Send catastrophic rains or veils
of vatic mist, or misspell my name in fallen pollen.

I'm not particular. Just help me know there's a *me*
inside this me, a *you* that licks like vitalizing fire.

After Canceling My Life Insurance

I feel lighter somehow, more aligned with fate,
with solstice, with the way maples mumble
in underground code then high-five the sky
when wind picks up. What a relief not
to be pickpocketed by Corporate same day
same place ever again. I nap at noon
and call that a premium, skip rocks and call
that a down payment on crayfish and eternity.
Let robins steal my apricots—why not?
Let slugs take out my cukes—how clever!
I crouch like Buddha when I change the cat
litter. Apologize to boxelder bugs before
slurping them off the window with a wand.
Time to take up a new kind of calculus:
how many monarchs per breeze, how many
breezes per cul-de-sac, knowing only a turkey
vulture floating above will understand
residuals. Time to mail a letter in town, time
to turn off the radio and take a shortcut home
behind Kroger. Cattails and cottonwoods.
Cottonwoods and broken grocery carts.
And in the middle of that mess, a heron.
I kill the engine and roll my window down
to grab a pic or two. Then stop. Why hoard
happy, why not just let it simmer? Go
somewhere else, I yell at that bird. We don't
deserve your electric blues and godly pliés.
Then I repeat *heron heron heron*, like some
kid dropping joyful F-bombs during church.

Flag Flying at Half-Staff over Woodland Hills Municipal Building

Someone has died but who—some crotchety
former VP, the mayor, Jane Goodall? I kill
my car radio as I drive by. My silence and the stars
and stripes flapping over dirty windows
and the town's only snowplow. What mystery!

Someone has died but who? I flip the radio
back on—Janis Joplin crooning. Let the flag
flap in honor of her voice raw as road rash.
And flap over the dead doe I just passed
and the 10,000 ants I'm plotting to snuff out.

Which is why I'm hitting Ace Hardware for bugicide.
I begged the colony to vacate my wife's studio,
but they refused to hold talks. What an advocate
I am for fresh gesso, what a lousy Buddhist!
Someone has died but who? Are we honoring

recent hurricane victims? The boot that washed
up in Vancouver, *ex nihilo*, with a foot still in it?
How about the dead smoldering in Gaza?
I'd love to invite both Palestinians and Israelis
to a solstice sleepover and pass around kettle corn.

But experts say, *Nope, you have to choose.* How
about choosing to build a castration machine
instead and inviting hawkish leaders to test-drive it?
If some whack-job general wants blood,
fine, but first let him give up something dear.

Let the machine crush or wield tiny knives.
Let war hounds (almost always men if you haven't
noticed) be castrated on live TV—naked,
without anesthetic, but with memes. Watch war
deaths plummet, watch peasants dance in the streets!

Cruel and unusual punishment? You bet.
But it would give me, give all of us, more time
to linger over unsung deaths in Shakespeare,
including Gertrude and Ophelia, poor girls.
Especially Ophelia. Whenever she takes her final

moony breath, I want to jump on stage and bring
her back with a kiss. Let's make that the lead
on the evening news. Someone has died but who?
I confess to killing ants but draw the line
at larger souls, like this flock of derelict turkeys

crossing the road, loony bobbing things
who don't always flee harm's way fast
enough. Like an Israeli boy offering a drink
of water to a dying soldier. Like a Palestinian girl
petting a whimpering dog behind its bloody ear.

Hospice

During those final hours, in the slow throes
of letting go, our mother smoldered on,

a dying campfire, and *Animal Planet*, sound off,
glowed from the corner like a broken star.

My sisters and I gargled stories, sipped soup,
hummed hymns we didn't know we knew.

Weird comfort to take Mom's hand and watch
a line of leafcutter ants carrying green sails

vanish into the welcoming earth. Or turn
towards her morphine snores and glimpse

manatees, agile as angels, doing flip turns
in the dark in the brine of that shallowy deep.

Hungry in the Hague

And now a waitress with a rose tattoo
on one calf and a lightning
bolt on the other is preparing to feed
the world dinner—or at least the seven
curbside tables entrusted to her care.
One plastic orchid per conversation,
one flame of eternity per meal.

It has rained, the sky glowing
a ragged blue, as if licked clean
and given a second lease on life.
The waitress, humming now,
sweeps and straightens.
A cat with a jinked tail laps
at a hosta leaf heavy with drips.

The sun skates from puddle to puddle.
My happiness angels are near
enough I can almost high-five them.
Let them linger, let them linger!
I hear the nestlings before I see them,
a scatter of scratchy chirrups
leaking from a nest tucked under

the eaves of the store next door.
Their golden beaks jab straight up.
Where oh where is our lost
mother? They're asking, I'm asking,
we've all been asking our entire hungry
lives, and we clack our soft beaks
to make the broken worms come faster.

Two Horses in a Field in Mid-December

These strands of twisting wires keeping horses
there and me here is called a fence. Tears
form and tears fall from above and we call
it rain. If it freezes, as it is doing now,
we name it snow, even if sun flares
from the east bright as sparkly postcards
from Colorado. And this patch of dead grass

hurtling through time and tomorrow equals
a blue sphere we call Earth. We rarely send Earth
thank-you notes. It is easier to worry
about spiced tea and poinsettias and our cousin's
accident and winter solstice and a late
mortgage payment and future trysts
and where in town one can buy decent focaccia.

My left hand is cold, my right hand colder,
and I wonder how long I can lean
on this fence watching it snow? The wet stuff
collects on the back of a white horse,
a matching blanket. It falls too on the back
of this black mare but dissolves.
This is how mystery and beauty collude,

how even a weak trickle of sun fills me
with awe. Tonight, I will look at the sky
and string pulsing stars into creatures
and call it astronomy. And I'll look inside
and see more broken creatures and call it
middle age, call it longing, call it
where are all the sweet rivers I used to swim?

I'll talk to the dark I'm walking through
and call it worship. I'll chew on it, sing cracked
psalms to it, even cough it out and pretend
it has no place in me. But that's for later.
Right now, colors are streaming through
this camera called the eye, starlings
flicking and flirting, flapping and finessing.

My hands are still cold, my breath vapor.
I alone lean into this field, this story problem
in stillness, one horse white, one black, a little
snow, a little sun. How long will Earth hold me
in its tender mouth? I count backwards from 100.
An orange cat weasels by. Robins scrap
over a rosehip. I have no idea what I'm counting.

Why I Petted the Cat

Because I was tired and cranky and it was too late
to take a bus to Siena and ask Saint Catherine's
mummified thumb to fix my insomnia.
Because Florence was threatening to rain
all over us, especially me. Did I mention
I was starving and that my wife wanted to visit
the *David* a second time? Because this cat
craved attention and because my impatient
American paws had to do something.
Not a Persian or Maltese, this charmer,
nor a fancy ebony number, just a motley calico.
That's a point in my favor, isn't it? Me trying
to love all mammals equally. Because my species
once grew hair everywhere. When petting,
begin with the ears and ugly cat head,
and don't forget the greedy chin. Sure,
I worried about distemper and Lyme disease
and feline herpes but not enough to stop.
Because I considered myself a back-alley
healer and amateur shaman. Because I liked
tracing the backbone, transferring lightning
from human hand to feline spine. Because
I liked tabling my usual quandaries—who
to choose first in fantasy soccer, da Vinci
or Michelangelo, and how to bribe God
into liking me again. Because I could tell
from the cat's beseeching eyes she was alone
in Italy, same as me, and spoke almost
no Italian. Because her purring was exquisite,
her swishing tail unregulated by Pope or police
or cloud. Because chaos was everywhere,
because I like the electric glow of a furry success.

I'm Done with Birds

After a week away to bury my mother, we found
robins nesting above our front door.
Was this a cosmic joke, one mother laid to rest,
a new mother bivouacking on the porch?
But what to do, move future chirps
to a nearby spruce, toss out five beating hearts?
In the end, we left the nest, and now we come
and go, like squatters, through the smelly garage.
But as soon as these fledglings fledge,
I'm placing a moratorium on birds.
No more feathers and bird crap in person,
and no more crooners sneaking into lines
where they don't belong. And no more
bird verbs. No *flapping* or *hopping*, no *soaring*
into ether or *diving* into the blue abyss
of an unplumbed lake. Out with hummingbirds
and house wrens, out with plover tracks
like hieroglyphs in the sand. And especially out
with nests. Weeks of brooding and hatching
and feeding above my door have worn me out.
Their nest is hope and death, mud and magnetic
tangles of an ancient cassette all at once.
Maybe Joni Mitchell, maybe Black Sabbath?
And still the chicks screech for more worms.
The world is made of calcium, hunger is a beak.
My bones hold broken time. My hands cup
grief. And the blue above just goes on and on.
My mother is gone, my mother is a ghost.
If she wants to haunt me, let her do it without
mourning doves and elegant floating hawks
to nudge her cause along. Let crickets serve
as delegates, let locusts guide her bravely home.

Thirty-One Views from the Hammock

1. Solstice, and still the maples flaunt their green tresses.

2. The smoky gossip of burning trash.

3. A mug of yesterday's tepid jasmine tea.

4. What passes as shade: the drifting jibber-jabber of clouds.

5. A hammock and a man are one.

6. A hammock and a man and his wife's shoulders are one.

7. Not her actual shoulders, which are in Cincinnati this week.

8. But his freckled memory of them.

9. Next door, a trampoline launches a boy into the blue.

10. Not on my watch, you don't, says gravity.

11. Visit again real soon, says the air.

12. Closer to earth, a fountain pleasures itself and gathers bees.

13. A mantis interviews a cricket, one bite at a time.

14. Sheets snapping in lavender praise.

15. The crime is not Bartók or the piano or little girl hands.

16. Blame the window, that busybody open window.

17. Poor ant: trundling home a moth as big as a sailboat.

18. Like much in life, wings are metaphor.

19. So many leaves, so many shivery prayers.

20. Free sky miles, says the sky—use them.

21. Distant thunder, like God reshelving books.

22. Will this pile of gravel ever become a path?

23. Do some angles of repose double as tipping points?

24. Whose tragedy does that dying car alarm usher in?

25. You call this a nap?

26. Questions like these—they keep chasing each other. Fit *man, hammock,* and *longing* into one sentence—never.

27. Why not? His beloved's shoulders won't hold still.

28. Do guardian angels choose whom they haunt?

29. Rain, some say, is an aphrodisiac.

30. Teach me, teach me tonight.

31. Inside, the teapot whistles, as if gathering our lost ones home.

Self-Portrait as Aspiring Mystic

I have no spooky mantras but I can whisper
Indie Indie Indie into the dark, praying coyotes
will spare my cat. I failed to see in the falls
gods letting down their fugitive hair,
but I rescued a turkey feather from dirt.
I don't know the color of my heart
chakra, but seven days running I've touched
my lucky desert rock holding the window open.
Can't erase mudslides but I can snatch
a mantis from the path of a lumbering bus.
In another life I might have advised the king,
mended nets, read the entrails of a slaughtered
sheep, or reached inside a mare's slippery
canal and turned the colt. In this life,
I'm a man with flat feet and splinted middle
finger who flips off scrambled eggs, staring
stars, and my beloved—all by accident.
Did I say I love this life? *Lord, how I love*
this life. In all its broken backfiring beauty.
Can't float on mist, but I can bag garbage
under a full moon. Can't quiet yammering
dogs, but I can dance. No prayers inside me
today, but I can flip over a board behind
my house and catalogue scattering shamans,
all wriggle and writhe, scurry and scheme.
Look at them teem. This one soft-shoeing
away on 100 legs, this one carrying venom
in its curling tail, this one cricketing with praise.

Advice to Myself

Your dad has been dead a decade, stop smuggling
him into lame lines about fly fishing and whetstones
gooped with spit. And stop using *crooked*
and *Tierra del Fuego* and eleven other words
you think you invented. Not enough baklava
or Turkish delight in your stanzas, not enough
faith in wabi-sabi, the wobbly milk stool
falling apart like paper-mâché left in the rain.
What is it with you and the Rolling Stones?
Instead praise ABBA and mostly mean it,
praise Chet Baker and his sleepy, knowing
iteration of "My Funny Valentine" long after
his teeth got knocked out. No more deer,
especially not ethereal does scissoring through
a clearing at dawn, evoking emotional slither
about something called "the numinous."
For mystery, describe the antler tree out back.
For jealousy, your high school buddy
streaking through the lunchroom in nothing
but sneakers and a striped balaclava.
For insult and inadequacy, the bald custodian
saying *long-haired sissy boys like you are wrecking*
this country. If nothing memorable floats
your way, quote Milosz's broken-down angel:
day draws near another one do what you can.
Then go change the cat litter. You haven't
been special since your third-grade spelling bee.
Stop crutching along on Nietzsche, and no
more images of St. Francis offering his cupped
hands to wounded wrens. Everyone's wounded,
get over it. Orpheus is fair game, but only
if you describe his cut-off head floating
down the Hebrus singing praises to lowing cows.

In My Next Life I'll Return as a Crow

Or raven or rook, I don't care, maybe a magpie,
something with black pin feathers,
a scrounger at heart. I'll eat eggs, fish, mice,
worms, and frogs. Also roadkill.
Also sweet potato fries smashed
in a truck stop parking lot, and I'll swallow
any clinging ants. Ah, that peppery crunch.

Am I the absence of color or all colors
mixed? I am a flung stone, the silence
that fills the space after each blasted
caw. I will pray by floating
on thermals, practice yoga by balancing
one-footed on the corpse of a dove.
Then carry my stingy heart across three deserts.

A crow's ethics lie in her talons and beak,
her empathy for whatever strange
fuel she can swallow. I will collect
trinkets just as I do in this life
only smaller—thimble, whistle, hairpins—
and measure immortality against
feather and bone and the sun going down.

I am one and I am many, one and whatever
I can steal. Too many of us to count?
A murder. I will hop from sadness
to sadness, every tree an audition
for a new horror film. If my lonely
rowing crosses paths with your children,
within ninety-nine years each will die.

I'll count my life in fenceposts, eat
the eye of a festering deer. Hikers
will cringe at my filthy flits, jeer
my cowardice, then hurry home to scrub
their sleek bodies, which touched golden
air which touched me. My trickster
ways already working inside them.

Acknowledgments

Thanks to the editors of the following magazines, journals, and other venues in which these poems first appeared:

32 Poems: "Thirty-One Views from the Hammock"
Alaska Quarterly Review: "After Canceling My Life Insurance"
Cincinnati Review: "AD&D"
Conduit: "Advice to Myself"
Irish Times: "Things I'm Against"
Lake Effect: "In My Next Life I'll Return as a Crow"
Missouri Review: "I'm Done with Birds" and "Lives of the Animals"
New Letters: "Interior Weather"
North American Review: "A Partial Accounting"
Poem-a-Day: "To My Daughter's Dead Name"
Rattle: "Dear First Draft of This Poem" and "Why I Petted the Cat"
Sewanee Review: "Two Horses in a Field in Mid-December"
Southern Review: "Hungry in the Hague"
Swamp Pink: "Secretary of the Invisible Thing"
The Sun: "Bring Me a Horse"
West Branch: "Custodian of Scat"
Witness: "Hospice"

"I'm Done with Birds" and "Lives of the Animals" are part of a suite of poems that won the 2024 Editor's Prize sponsored by the *Missouri Review*.

"Things I'm Against" won *The Moth* Poetry Prize in 2024 (Ireland).

"Secretary of the Invisible Thing" won the 2023 *Swamp Pink* (formerly *Crazyhorse*) Prize.

"Two Horses in a Field in Mid-December" won the 2021 *Sewanee Review* Prize.

"Dear First Draft of This Poem" was a finalist for the 2024 Rattle Poetry Prize.

Two poems were recently reprinted: "Thirty-One Views from the Hammock" in *Tree Lines: 21st Century American Poems* and "Two Horses in a Field in Mid-December" in *Poetry Daily* and *The Color Wheel.*

Thanks once again to my usual co-conspirators: Susan Howe, Michael Lavers, Scott Hatch, Steve Tuttle, and Spencer Hyde. Deep gratitude to Timothy Green and everyone at *Rattle.* Thanks to the College of Humanities and the English Department at Brigham Young University for providing me time to write, and to colleagues and students for keeping me honest. And special thanks to Jacqui Larsen, first reader always.

About the Rattle Chapbook Series

The Rattle Chapbook Series publishes and distributes a chapbook to all of *Rattle*'s print subscribers along with each quarterly issue of the magazine. Most selections are made through the annual Rattle Chapbook Prize competition (deadline: January 15th). For more information, and to order other chapbooks from the series, visit our website.

2026 | *Secretary of the Invisible Thing* by Lance Larsen
The Soft Black Stars by Matthew Buckley Smith
2025 | *no matter how it ends a bluebird's song* by Kat Lehmann
Haunt Me by José Enrique Medina
Backlit by Liz Robbins
2024 | *Cheap Motels of My Youth* by George Bilgere
In Which by Denise Duhamel
Sky Mall by Eric Kocher
2023 | *The Fight Journal* by John W. Evans
At the Car Wash by Arthur Russell
Plucked by Miracle Thornton
2022 | *Imago, Dei* by Elizabeth Johnston Ambrose
The Morning You Saw a Train of Stars ... by CooXooEii Black
Visiting Her in Queens Is More Enlightening ... by Michael Mark
2021 | *The Death of a Migrant Worker* by Gil Arzola
A Plumber's Guide to Light by Jesse Bertron
I Will Pass Even to Acheron by Amanda Newell
2020 | *Adjusting to the Lights* by Tom C. Hunley
A Juror Must Fold in on Herself by Kathleen McClung
Falling off the Empire State Building by Jimmy Pappas
2019 | *The Last Mastodon* by Christina Olson
Hansel and Gretel Get the Word on the Street by Al Ortolani
Did You Know? by Elizabeth S. Wolf
2018 | *To Those Who Were Our First Gods* by Nickole Brown
Tales from the House of Vasquez by Raquel Vasquez Gilliland
Punishment by Nancy Miller Gomez
A Bag of Hands by Mather Schneider
2017 | *In America* by Diana Goetsch
The Whetting Stone by Taylor Mali
2016 | *3arabi Song* by Zeina Hashem Beck

www.**Rattle**.com